Easy Classical Guitar Duets

Easy Classical Guitar Duets
Arranged and edited by JAVIER MARCÓ

Easy Classical Guitar Duets
© 2011 by Javier Marcó. All Rights Reserved. International Copyright Secured.
© 2011 Cover Photographs by Eugenia Pereyra. All Rights Reserved.

ISBN-13:978-1463776947
ISBN-10:1463776942

Unauthorized reproduction of any part of this publication by any means including photocopying is an infringement of copyright.

Contents

Playing guide 7

1812 Overture 14

A Little Night Music 16

The Blue Danube 19

Bridal Chorus 22

Canon in D 24

Dance of the Flowers 28

Für Elise 30

Greensleeves 33

In the Hall of the Mounain King 36

La Donna é Mobile 38

Land of Hope and Glory 40

Lullaby 42

Ode to Joy 44

Spring - Four Seasons 46

Playing guide

Notation
In this book, two methods of music notation are presented: standard notation and tablature.

Tablature
Tablature indicates the position of the notes on the fretboard. There are six lines, one for each string.

1 Thinest
STRINGS
6 Thickest

The number placed on a line indicates the fret location of a note.

This indicates the 3rd fret of the first string: a G note.

This indicates the 1st fret of the second string: a C note.

This indicates the third string open: a G note.

This indicates the 4th fret of the fourth string: an F# note.

This indicates the 5th fret of the fifth string: a D note.

This indicates the sixth string open: an E note.

Standard notation
Notes are written on a Staff.

Staff
The staff consists of five lines and four spaces, on which notes symbols are placed.

Clef
A clef assigns an individual note to a certain line. The **Treble Clef** or **G Clef** is used for the Guitar.

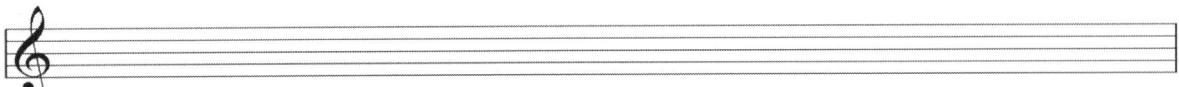

This clef indicates the position of the note G which is on the second line from the bottom.

Note
A note is a sign used to represent the relative pitch of a sound. There are seven notes: A, B, C, D, E, F and G.

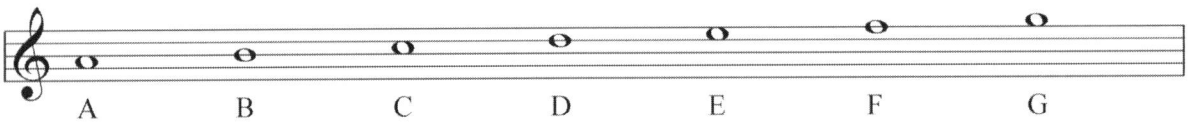

Ledger lines
The ledger lines are used to inscribe notes outside the lines and spaces of the staff.

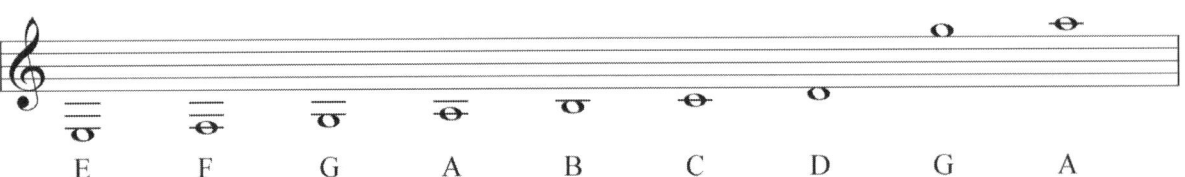

Accidentals
An accidental is a symbol to raise or lower the pitch of a note.

♯ sharp   Next note up half step.

♭ flat   Next note down half step.

♮ natural   Cancels a flat or a sharp.

8

Note values

A **note value** is used to indicate the duration of a note. A **rest** is an interval of silence, marked by a sign indicating the length of the pause. Each rest corresponds to a particular note value.

𝅝	Whole note	𝄻	Whole rest
𝅗𝅥	Half note	𝄼	Half rest
𝅘𝅥	Quarter note	𝄽	Quarter rest
𝅘𝅥𝅮	Eight note	𝄾	Eight rest
𝅘𝅥𝅯	Sixteenth note	𝄿	Sixteenth rest

Dotted note

A dotted note is a note with a small dot written after it. The dot adds half as much again to the basic note's duration.

Tie

A tie is a curved line connecting the heads of two notes of the same pitch, indicating that they are to be played as a single note with a duration equal to the sum of the individual notes' note values.

Bars or Measures

The staff is divided into equal segments of time consisting of the same number of beats, called bar or measures.

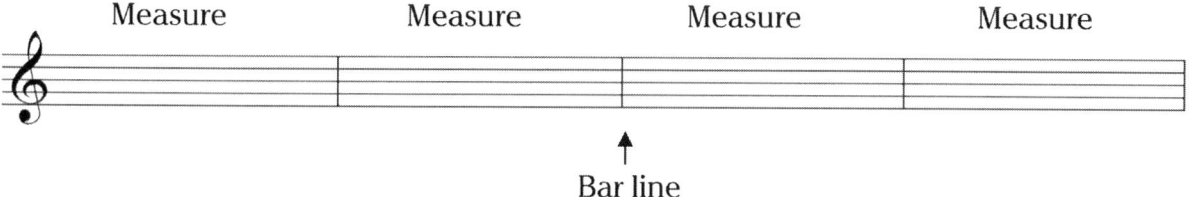

Bar line

Time signature

Time signature consists of two numbers, the upper number specifies how many beats (or counts) are in each measure, and the lower number tells us the note value which represents one beat.

Example: 4/4 means four quarters, or four beats per measure with a quarter note receiving one beat or count.

Key signature
A Key signature is a group of accidentals, generally written at the beginning of a score immediately after the clef, and shows which notes always get sharps or flats. Accidentals on the lines and spaces in the key signature affect those notes throughout the piece unless there is a natural sign.

Repeat sign
The repeat sign indicates a section should be repeated from the beginning, and then continue on. A corresponding sign facing the other way indicates where the repeat is to begin.

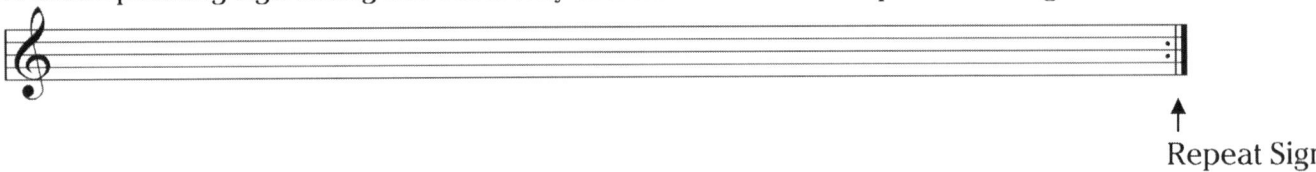

↑ Repeat Sign

First and second endings
The section should be repeated from the beginning, and number brackets above the bars indicate which to played the first time (1), which to play the second time (2).

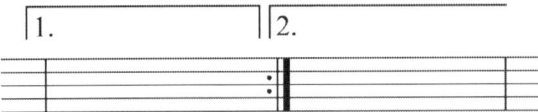

Fingering
In this book **left hand fingering** is indicated using numbers above the staff.
0= open
1= index
2= middle
3= ring
4= little finger

Right hand fingering
p= thumb
I = index
m=middle
a = ring

-Roman numbers indicates fret position for bars
CI = full bar, first fret.
cII = half bar, second fret.
Solid lines indicates how long to hold the bar.

Dynamics
Dynamics refers to the volume of the notes.

p   (piano), meaning soft.
mp   (mezzo-piano), meaning "moderately soft".
mf   (mezzo-forte), meaning "moderately loud".
f   (forte), meaning loud.

Crescendo. A gradual increase in volume.

Decrescendo. A gradual decrease in volume.

Tempo Markings
Tempo is written at the beginning of a piece of music and indicates how slow or fast this piece should be played.

Lento — very slow (40–60 bpm)
Adagio — slow and stately (66–76 bpm)
Andate — at a walking pace (76–108 bpm)
Moderato — moderately (101-110 bpm)
Allegro — fast, quickly and bright (120–139 bpm)
Allegretto — moderately fast (but less so than allegro)
Alla marcia — in the manner of a march
In tempo di valse — in tempo of vals

rallentando — gradual slowing down
a tempo — returns to the base tempo after a *rallentando*

Articulation

Legato. Notes are played smoothly and connected.

Stacatto. Notes are played separated or detached from its neighbours by a silence.

Fermata (pause)
The note is to be prolonged at the pleasure of the performer.

1812 Overture

Pyotr Ilyich Tchaikovsky
Arr. by Javier Marcó

Alla Marcia

A Little Night Music

Allegro

Wolfang Amadeus Mozart
Arr. by Javier Marcó

The Blue Danube

Johann Strauss
Arr. by Javier Marcó

Tempo di valse

Bridal Chorus

Richard Wagner
Arr. by Javier Marcó

Allegro

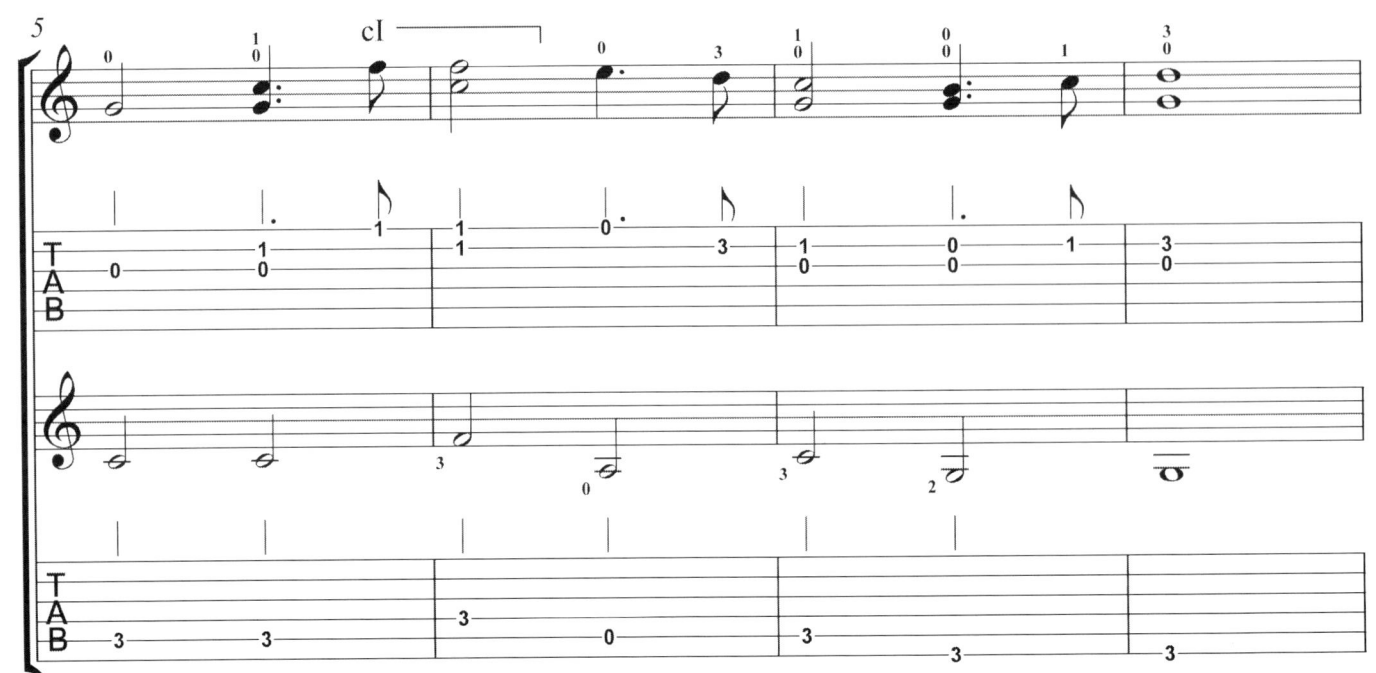

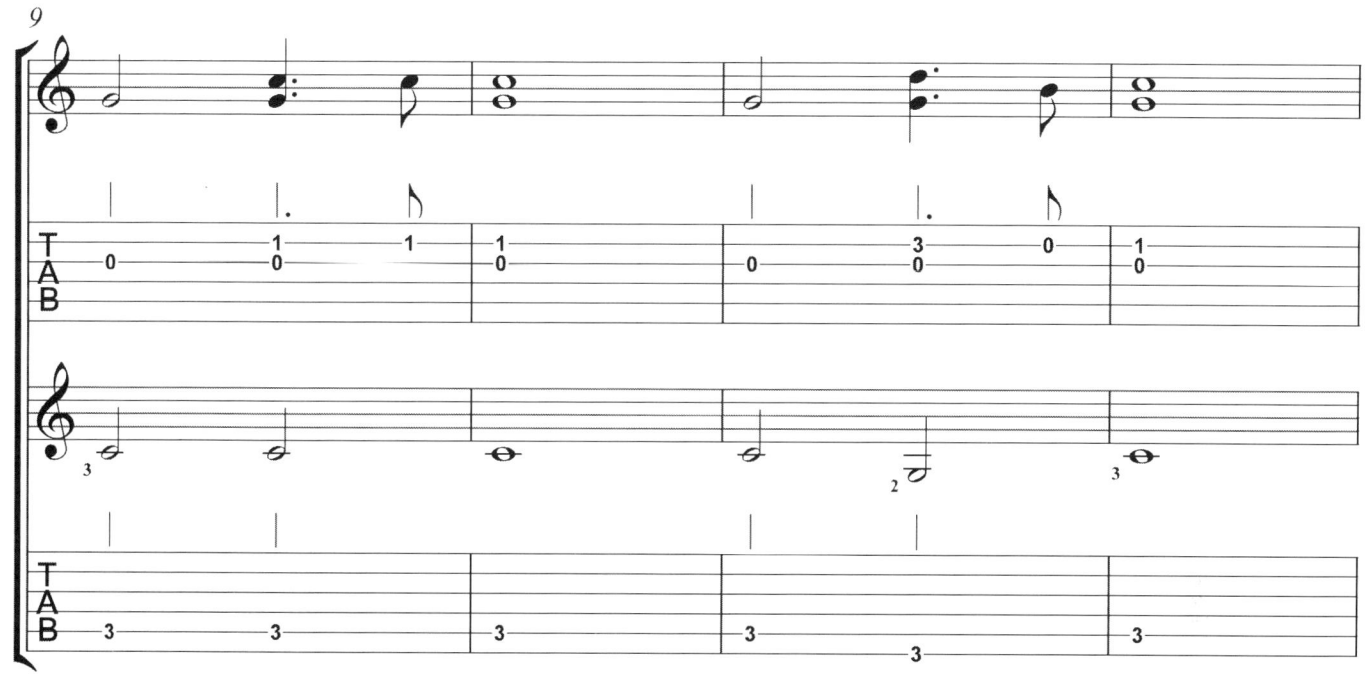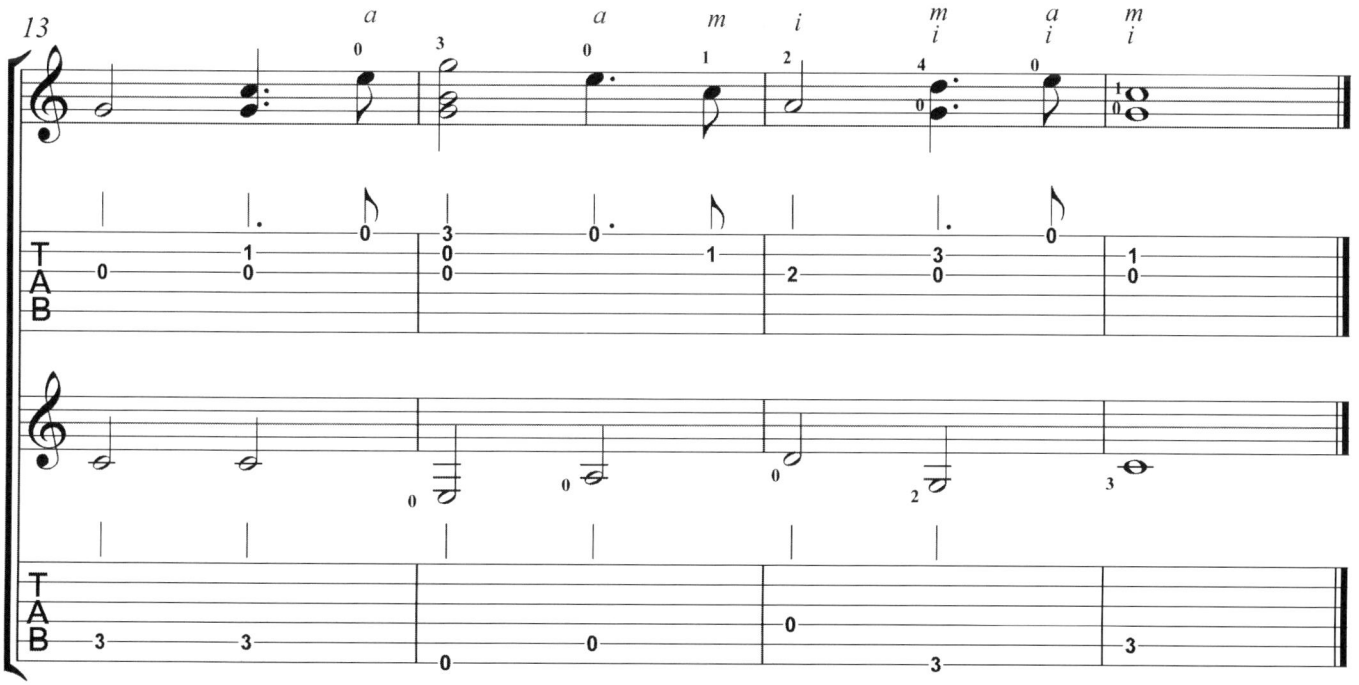

Canon in D

Johannes Pachelbel
Arr. by Javier Marcó

Adagio

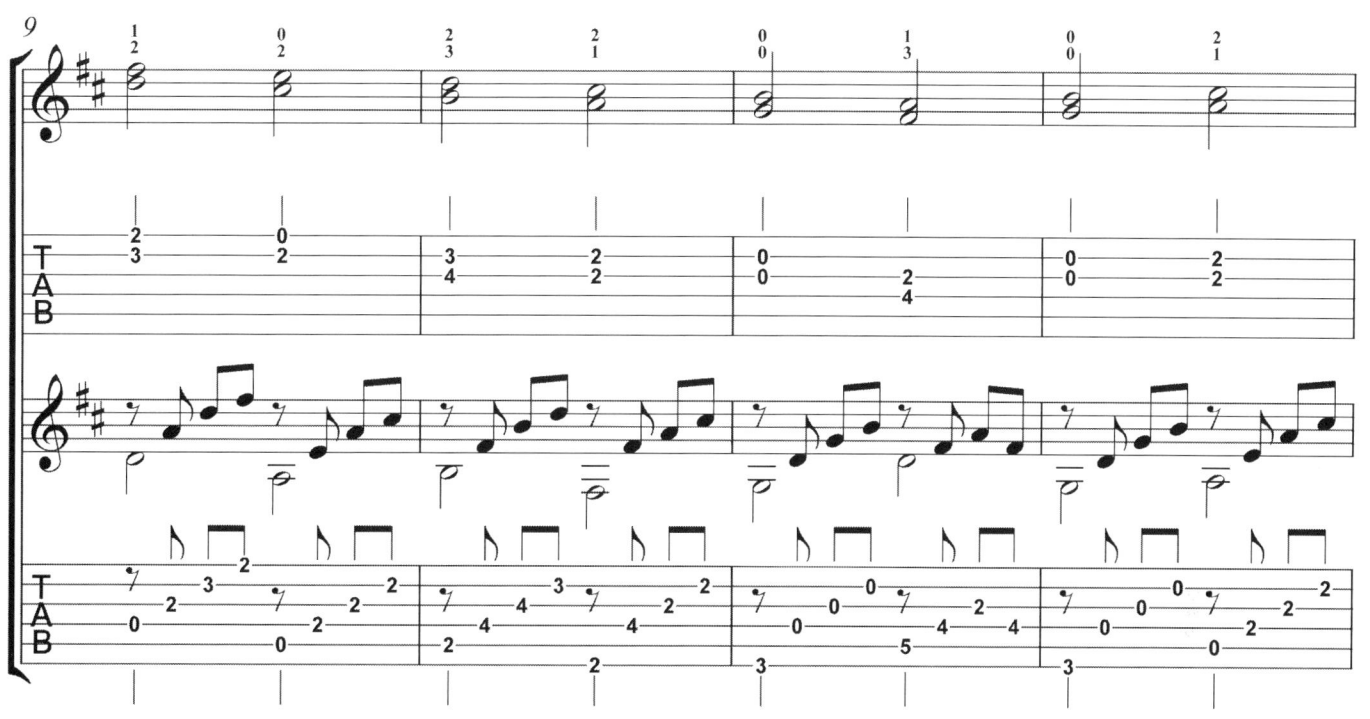

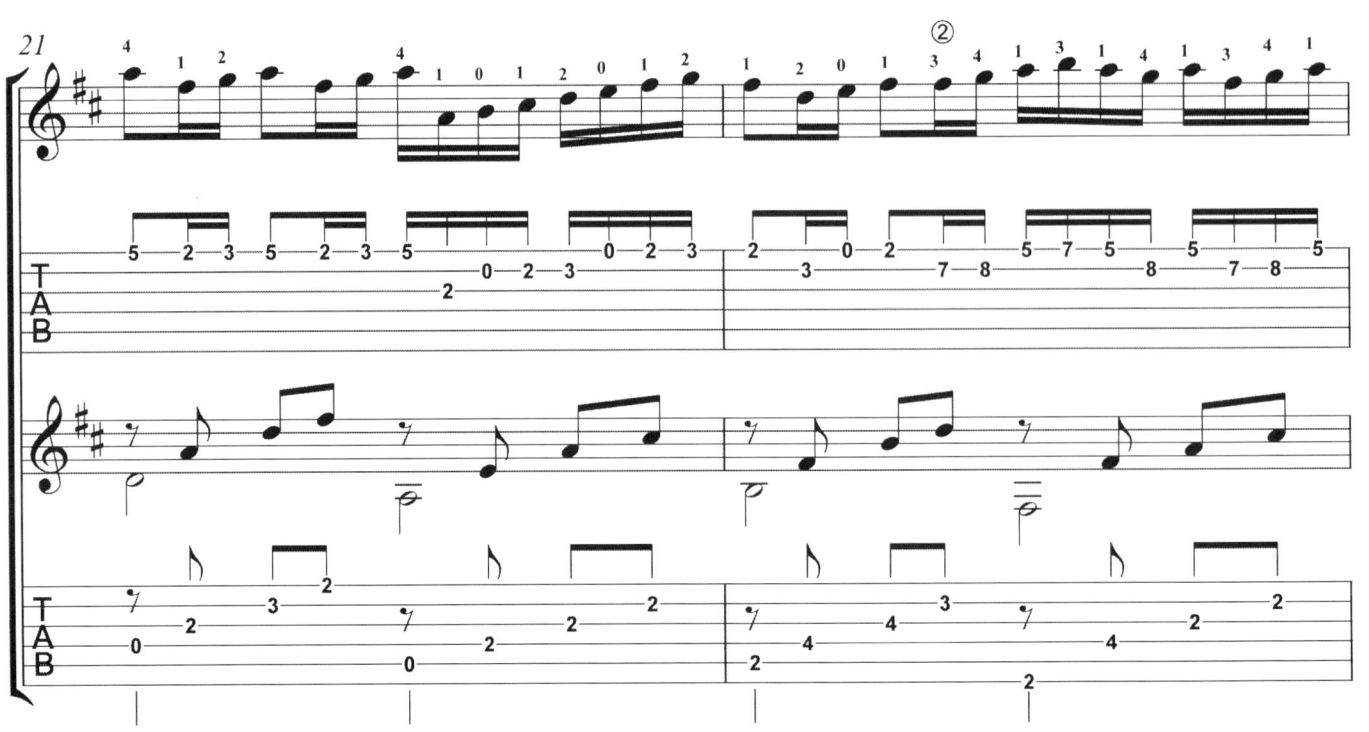

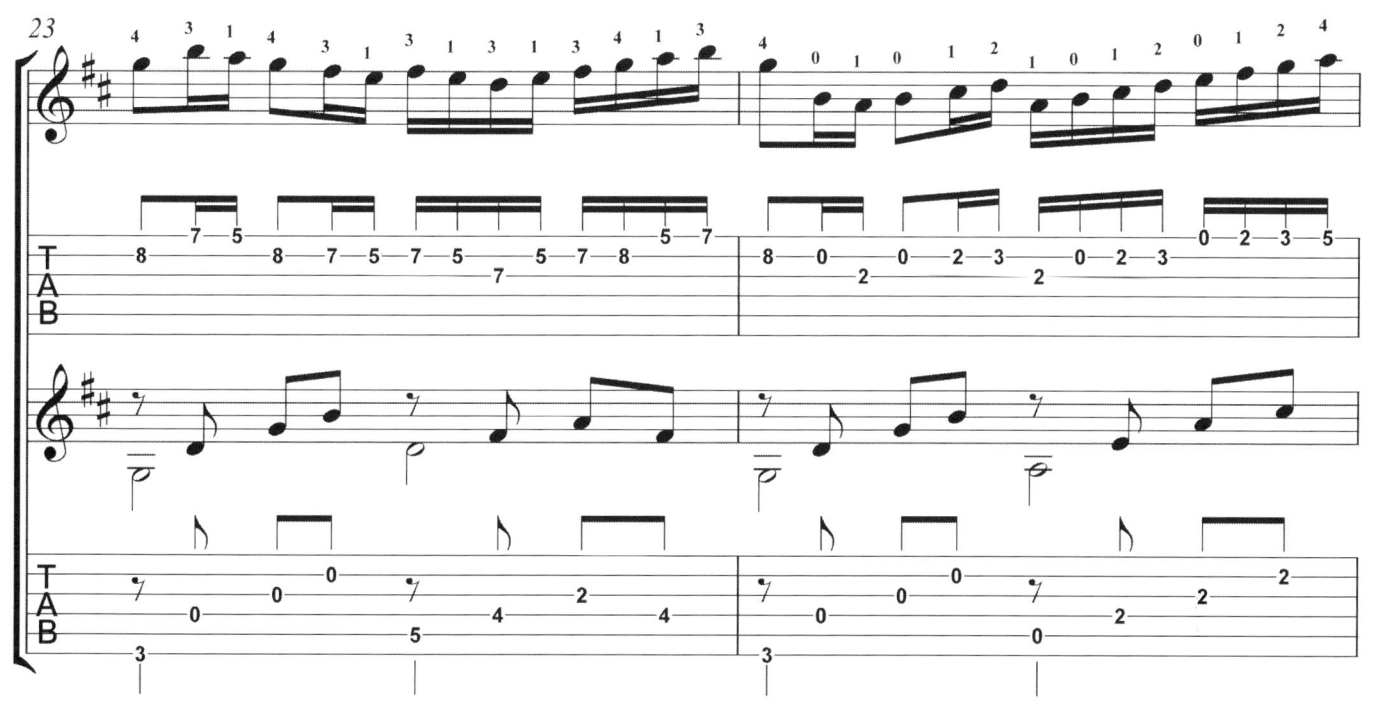

Dance of the Flowers

Pyotr Ilyich Tchaikovsky
Arr. by Javier Marcó

Tempo di valse

29

Für Elise

Ludwig Van Beethoven
Arr. by Javier Marcó

Poco Moto

Greensleeves

Anonymous
Arr. by Javier Marcó

Andante

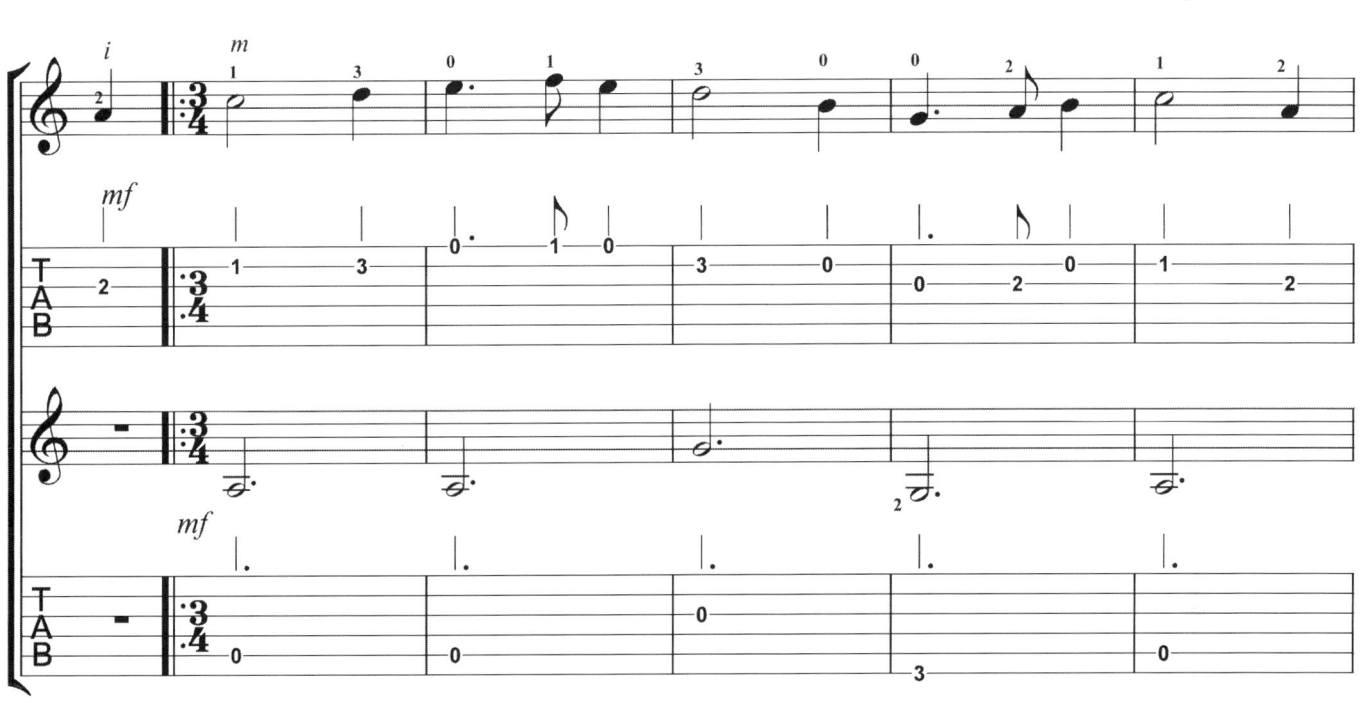
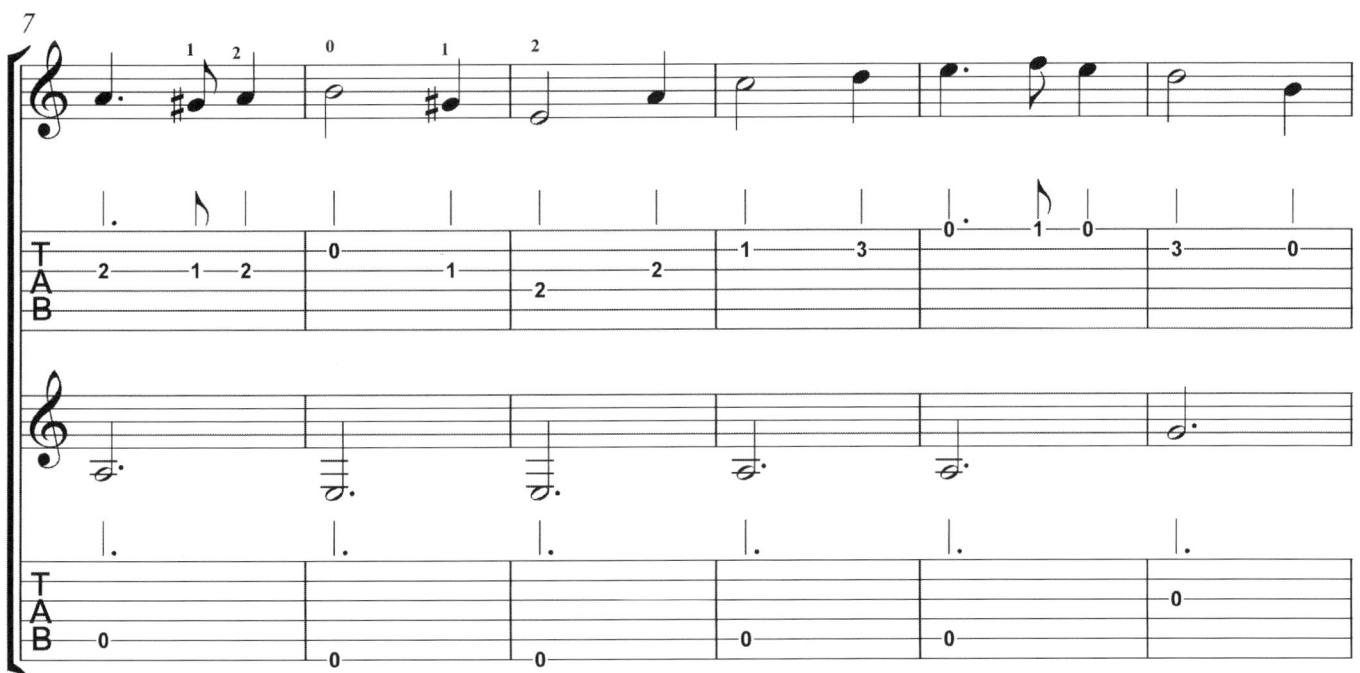

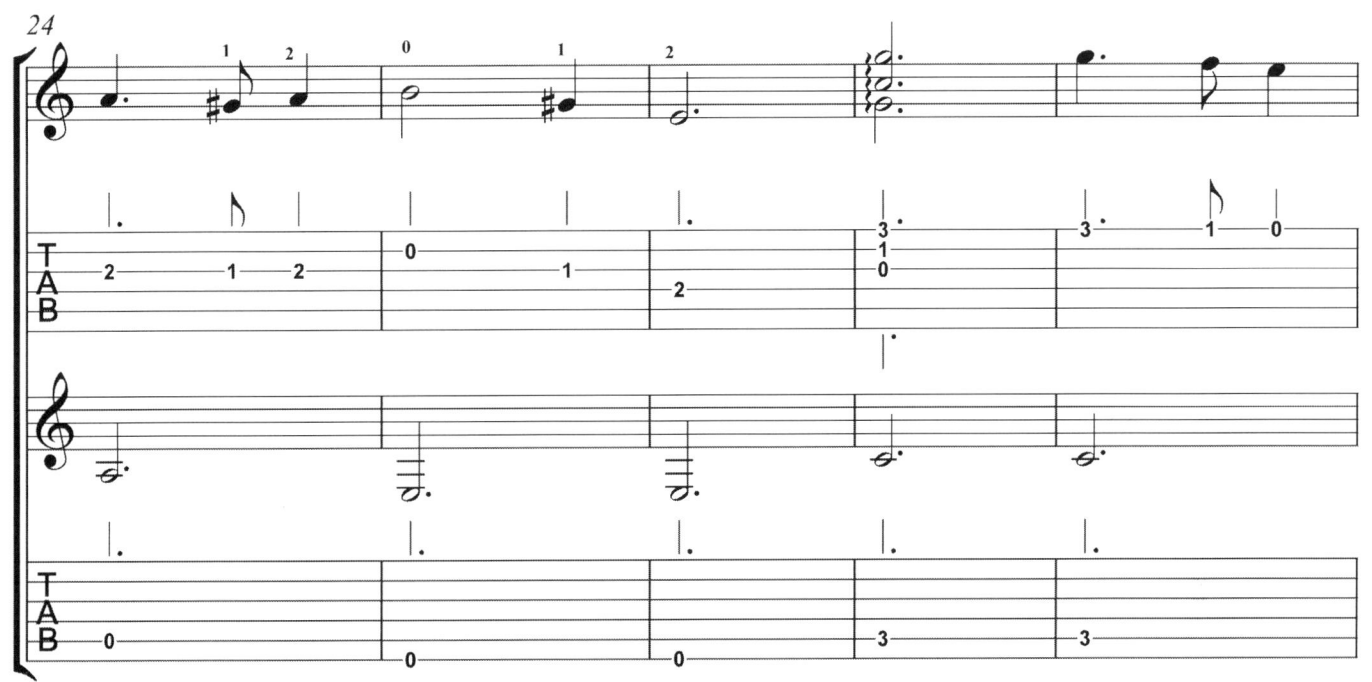

In the Hall of the Mountain King

Edgar Grieg
Arr. by Javier Marcó

Alla marcia e molto marcato

La Donna è Mobile

Giuseppe Verdi
Arr. by Javier Marcó

Allegro

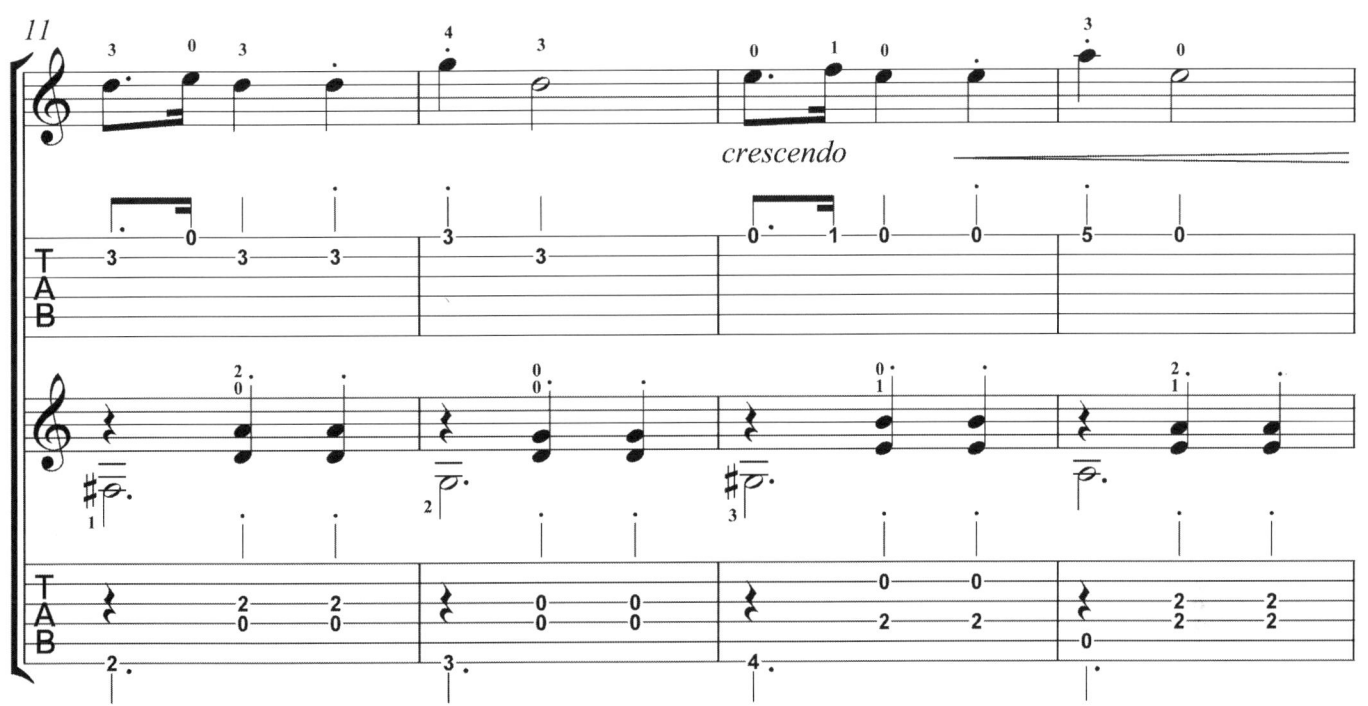

Land Of Hope And Glory

Edward Elgar
Arr. by Javier Marcó

Alla marcia, maestoso

Lullaby

Johannes Brahms
Arr. by Javier Marcó

Adagio

43

Ode to Joy

Ludwig Van Beethoven
Arr. by Javier Marcó

Moderato

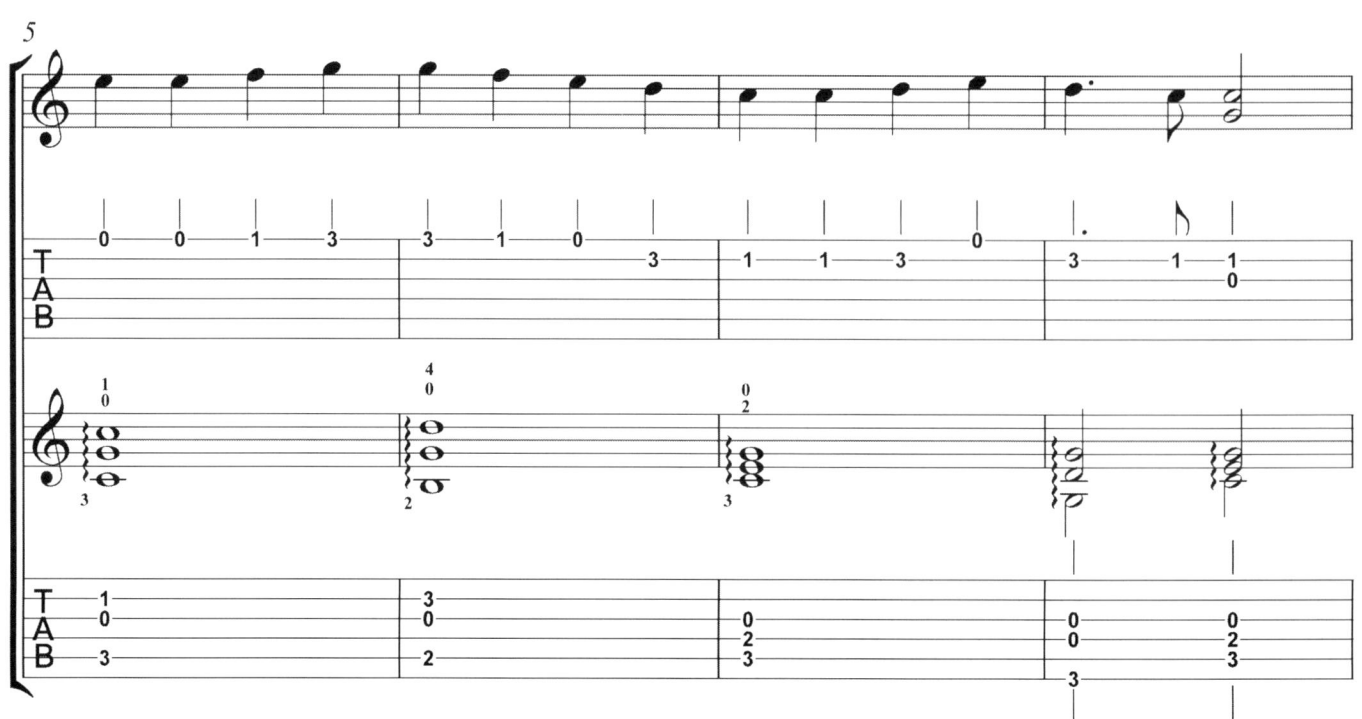

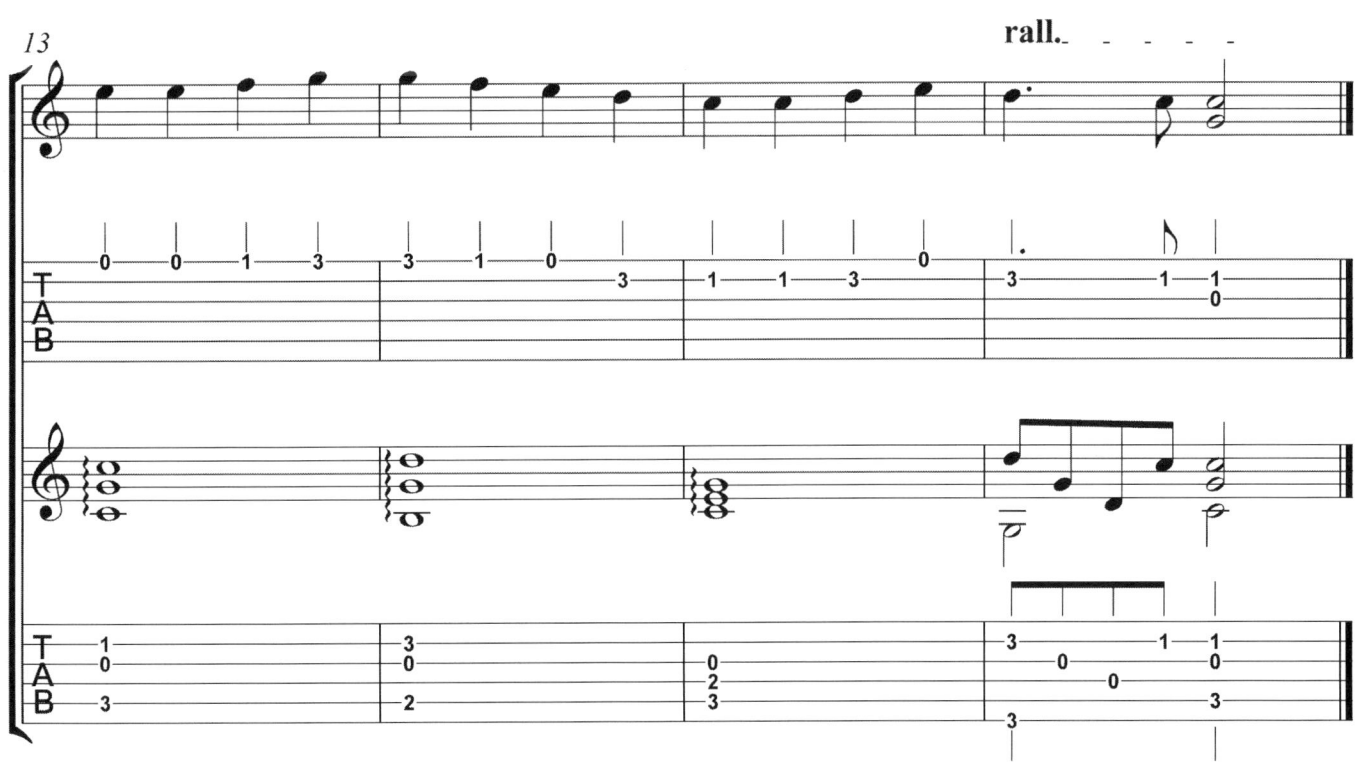

Spring - Four Seasons

Antonio Vivaldi
Arr. by Javier Marcó

Moderato

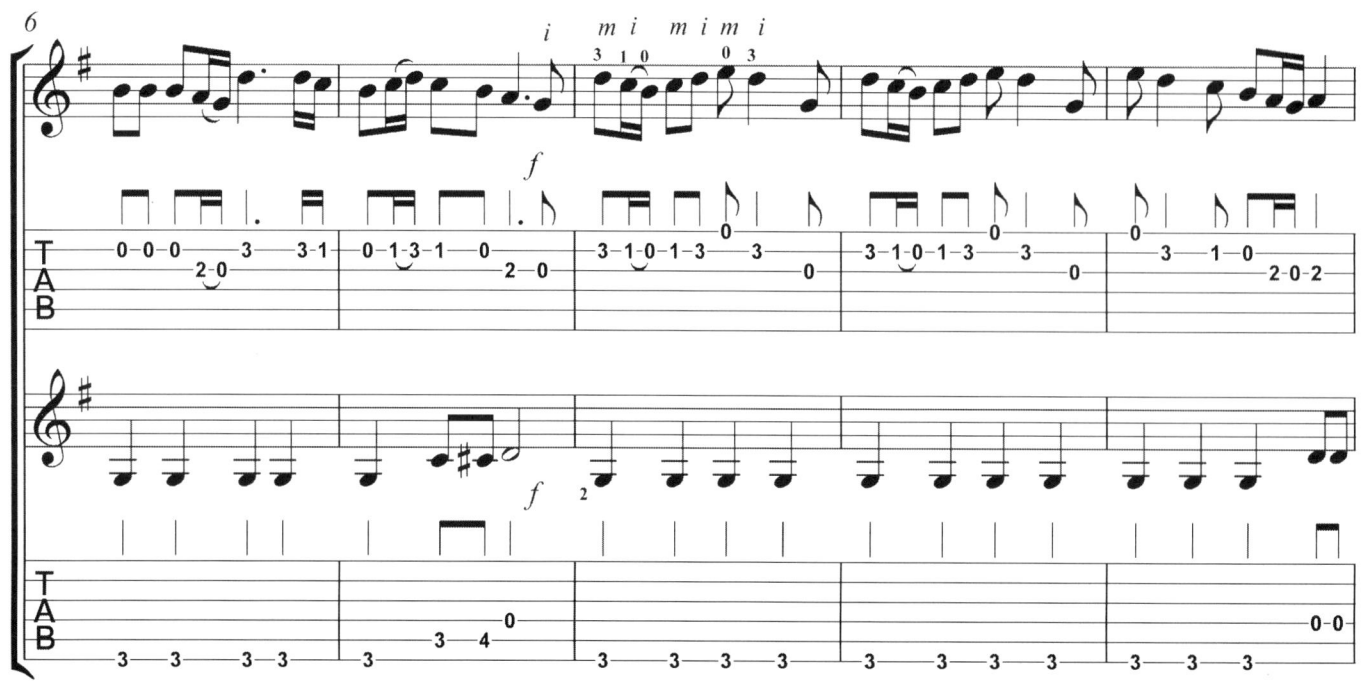

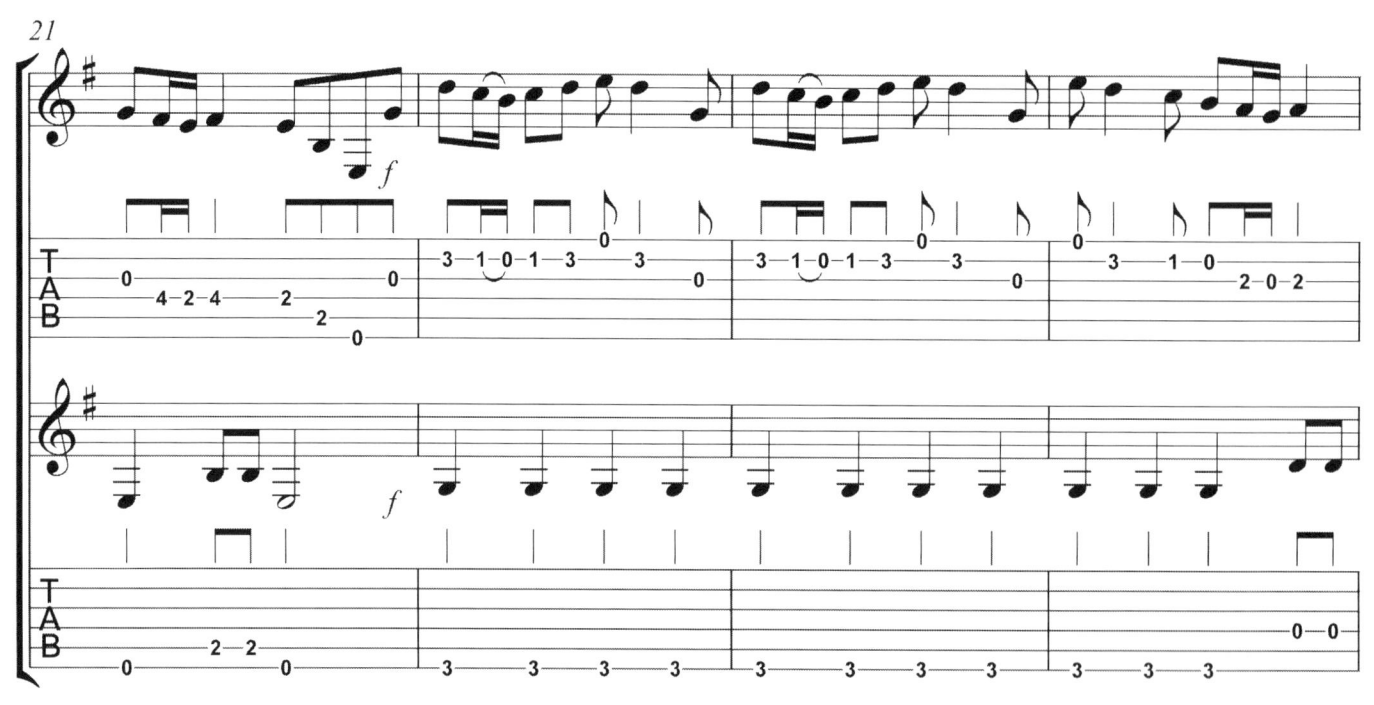

Other books in this collection:

For more info please visit our website:

www.marcomusica.com

Made in the USA
Middletown, DE
05 February 2015